Opening the Gate

Stories & Activities about Athletes with Disabilities

-Written for Young People-

Ingrid Floyd

Opening the Gate

Stories & Activities about Athletes with Disabilities

Life Skills Through Sports Series

Second Edition

Copyright © 2015

All Rights Reserved

Printed and Bound in the United States of America

Cover photo courtesy of Adaptive Sports Association of Durango, Colorado. Cover design by Alan Tsao. Hannah McFadden photo courtesy of Deborah McFadden. Beep baseball image courtesy of John Lykowski. Kevin Laue image courtesy of Manhattan College. Photo of Greg Gontaryk courtesy of Robert Memory. Jessica Tatiana Long photo courtesy of Jessica Tatiana Long. Cartoon by Rebekka Hearl.

Dedicated to our families -
their love and support
have meant so much to us.
Thank You!

Table of Contents

PREFACE

ABOUT THE COVER

SECTION I	THE ATHLETES	1
	Kevin Clinton Laue *The Hoop is as High as You Want It*	3
	Nicholas Ryan Taylor *The Garage Door to Success*	13
	Jessica Tatiana Long *Slicing through the Water with Humor*	21
	Hannah Vjollca McFadden *Train with the Heart of a Diamond*	29
	Greg Gontaryk *The Tech Talk of a Baseball*	37
	Anthony Netto *A Hole-in-One with Disabilities in Sports*	45
	Super Athlete *A Cartoon*	54
SECTION II	THE ACTIVITIES	57
	Hold a Carnival: *Support our Athletes with Disabilities*	59
	A Matching Card Game, *Know the Disabilities*	73
	What is it Like to Have a Disability in Sports?	79
SECTION III	FURTHER INFORMATION	85
	Ways to Adapt Sports for Athletes with Disabilities	87
	Quotes about Disabilities *from Athletes & Others*	91
	Web sites	93
ACKNOWLEDGMENTS		97
ABOUT US		98

Preface

Many sports books for young people focus on skills that are required for specific games, or recount the lives of famous athletes. These books are important, but by contrast, our bookstores and libraries lack material for young people, which emphasizes the broader life skills we can learn from sports. Many sports – from soccer to gymnastics to volleyball – can teach children valuable lessons that will prepare them to tackle life's difficult moments and nurture in them outstanding values to be used both on and off the field.

As a journalist with 30 years' experience working with young people, I decided to create a series of books with these lessons in mind. I conducted interviews with Paralympic, Olympic, professional, and college athletes and coaches about their experiences and the life skills they have learned. The stories are accompanied by hands-on paper and pencil activities, quotations and online resources, to teach young people the lessons that can be learned from the athletes themselves.

This first book, *Opening the Gate,* introduces youth to the world of wheelchairs and prostheses. Outstanding athletes, such as Nick Taylor, Hannah McFadden, Jessica Long, Kevin Laue, Anthony Netto, and Greg Gontaryk, recount the experiences that helped them participate effectively in sports and led them to the top of their athletic careers. The activities portion of this book provides ideas on how young people might host a fundraiser carnival for sports organizations that work with individuals with disabilities. Some of the carnival stations include wheelchair basketball, bowling for those who are visually impaired and a sit-down volleyball game. Another fun activity is a card game that teaches various medical terms about athletes' conditions. You will also find activities designed to help young people relate to the experience of the athlete with disabilities. At the end of the book, you can learn how to adapt sports for the individual with disabilities, relevant websites and inspirational quotations.

Many people contributed to this book, all believing children can learn from what they read and practice afterwards. From the beginning, my colleague Tom Bartsch, provided special help and was involved throughout the book's development. Together, we hope to inspire youth with disabilities and show them that there are many avenues they can take to enrich their lives through sport. For children who have no physical disabilities, our wish is that after reading this book, they will watch competitions for those with disabilities with excitement and come to better understand their brothers and sisters. It should help them grasp how able those with disabilities are.

Some people who heard our title, *Opening the Gate,* asked why we chose that name for this book. We did it for three reasons. First, a gate is associated with the "gateway to heaven" and with fulfilling a dream. These athletes with disabilities have been reaching for their own heaven. Second, Nick Taylor mentions in his story that in the old days, most of the gates to the tennis courts were too narrow for wheelchairs to enter. As our society is becoming more aware of the needs of the individuals with disabilities, we are widening these gates and creating access to all sorts of sports for athletes with disabilities. Lastly, the athletes are now opening up their lives, or "gates," to children who have not previously understood their struggles. *Opening the Gate* is therefore a natural title for this book.

We hope you enjoy learning from this book as much as we enjoyed researching and writing it.

Ingrid Floyd

Watch out for the next book in the series on character education.

About the Cover

Braxton Cole Perez, is a skier with Down syndrome - a fighter like the athletes with disabilities in the book. Cole was born on March 6, 1998, in Phoenix, Arizona, and now lives in Durango, Colorado, with his parents, Scott Perez and Patricia Sanders-Perez. From an early age, he loved playing baseball and soccer; but at age 11, he suffered a major stroke, losing use of both halves of his cerebellum. The neurologist told Cole's family he would have only as much as 48 hours to live, that he could not function without this part of the brain. But Cole surprised everyone, and was in a coma for only three days. When he awoke, his father, Scott, played Bruce Springsteen, Cole's favorite artist. Scott says, "Even when he was strapped to the table, he was moving his toes and fingers to the beat of the music. He just spreads lots of joy."

After the stroke, Cole lost balance, coordination, strength, and control of his muscles. He had to learn to walk and run again, and still is very awkward in these areas. It does not seem to bother him.

Cole knows his own limitations. "He just assumed things were going to be hard," his mother says. "He was like an infant again who had to relearn everything." For two years after the stroke, he used a feeding tube because he could not swallow liquids. He needed to retrain his muscles to chew. It took him five years before his speech started to return, leading to angry bouts and crying with frustration over not being able to communicate well to others. He had different fears than before, and still does. Shrill noises bothered him. Before fish did not scare him. Now they do. But with all these problems, he loves people and is thoughtful of them. In Durango, the students at his high school love him, and use body language to communicate with him. He knows 90 percent of them. He is on the cheerleading squad – 16 to 17 girls and Cole. He is the greatest cheerer. "Go Cole!" The fans cry. He is on the stage crew and loves schoolwork, except handwriting, which he refuses to do. He takes part in school events as much as he can. Patricia makes sure of it. Upon graduating, he wants to work for the scenic railroad; the owner plans to give him a job.

His favorite sport is skiing. It took tremendous effort and pain to get back on skis after the stroke, but he was patient. His past skiing trainer, Blair Ruder, who he adores, says that Cole would work hard to put on his boots for 45 minutes after the stroke. Because he had not learned to relax his ankles yet, she knew it had to hurt. He cried, but persevered. Cole was helped in skiing by adaptive equipment, but gradually used them less and less.

His mother says that it is a big deal when Cole reaches the bottom of the hill. She says, "Cole wants everyone to clap when he arrives. He throws up his hands and cheers." Blair says, "No one shows excitement like Cole." But Cole has his low periods. Blair says, "He is an authentic human being with emotions. He has many dimensions of his personality."

Not only is he gregarious and quiet but also compassionate and sensitive, as well. His father, Scott, says that Cole "knows how to bring both adults and children out of a funk." At a camping trip, Cole saw that a girl was alone and upset, so he went over and put his arm around her. She rested her head against his and cried. He said nothing, and she felt better. What would Scott say that Cole would advise a middle grader struggling with a problem, "No matter the issue you face, you can overcome it." Cole proves it every day. He would not give up, even when the odds were against him. Neither should you.

Opening the Gate

Section I

The Athletes

Hannah Vjollca McFadden

Kevin Clinton Laue

Anthony Netto

Greg Gontaryk

Jessica Tatiana Long

Nicholas Ryan Taylor

Section I The Athletes

Kevin Clinton Laue
The Hoop is as High as You Want It

Kevin Laue image courtesy
of Manhattan College.

Cameras flashed as Kevin Clinton Laue strode down the basketball court with his long, lanky legs and popped another ball into the net. The crowd erupted. To everyone, Kevin was something else. No one had seen anybody like him, for Kevin had only one arm. He was the first ever basketball player with one arm to land on a Division I team in college.

Section I The Athletes

Word about him reverberated around the world. President George W. Bush invited the 6'11 center aboard Air Force One. He was in *Sports Illustrated.* Franklin Martin even filmed a movie documentary on Kevin, called *Long Shot: The Kevin Laue Story,* which received excellent reviews.

Italian and Spanish reporters wrote articles. In 2008, an International Buddhist magazine in China featured Kevin. Two Brazilian news crews competed to air his story. One of the stations told him he was huge in Brazil for two weeks after the segment aired.

Kevin had reached his dream of playing on a top-level university team. He only wished that when the public viewed him on court, they would see him less as a special basketball player with one arm and more as an excellent basketball player.

After all, was there not more to the story of Kevin? Why was he so great? All his life, Kevin had been in the spotlight, but was the disability his story? Kevin learned the hard way that, in part, it always would be. He must deal with his disability as his own public relations man.

He knew it at 7 years old. He would tell his peers this story: "I was surfing on the island of Hawaii when the meanest creature in the sea, with these sharp, pointed teeth came chasing after me. It smelled the taste of my body. I could see his bloodthirsty eyes. It was a great bad big shark! It circled me. Before I knew it, the horrible creature had bitten off a chunk of my arm as I lurched away. My body writhed in pain." Kevin would watch all his onlookers open their mouths wide and their eyes pop. Then he would grin brightly and say, "Just kidding" and laugh. He loved recounting that story to others, and each time it was bigger, with more gestures.

Kevin did not lose his arm to a shark bite. It was just an elaborate tale his grandmother or mother, whomever you asked first, had told him to tell the kids who kept aggravating him by always asking, "Why do you have only one arm?" Telling it relieved him. He got tired of answering all their questions about why he was different from them.

But the truth about Kevin's arm would have been as fantastic as the shark story, if the 7-year-olds could have understood it. When Kevin was in his mother's womb, the umbilical cord that fed him his mother's nutrients had twisted around his neck en route to his navel. The cord pinned his arm against his neck, cutting off the blood flow and essentially "killing" the arm. But interestingly enough, the arm wedged under the cord saved Kevin's life because it prevented the cord from strangling Kevin's neck. Kevin's arm ends just below the elbow in a mass of scar tissue. Kevin likes to call it "The Nub," which he uses to assist him in holding a basketball after catching a pass in his favorite game.

Youngsters just thought Kevin's arm was something to make fun of. Since Kevin was born, they have taunted him, mocked him and rejected him. They have stared, whispered, and pointed fingers at him. They have called him, "Captain Hook," "One-Armed Jack" or "Lefty." Kevin to this day does not know what "One-Armed Jack" refers to. Is it from a movie or a book? Anyway, it made Kevin lose patience with them and doubt himself. Why could his peers not see that he was just like them? He had thoughts, feelings, drive, and talents, too. Think about it. Wouldn't it make you mad if your peers did that to you? You would hate it.

He was fortunate enough to live in a community where he went to school with the same kids throughout his elementary years, so they got used to his condition. But days could be difficult. You would think that by middle school, teenagers would have seen others with disabilities, but Kevin fared no better. Even though he was tall for his age, at 5'10 inches, many of the kids ridiculed him - not to his face,

Section I   The Athletes

because of his size - but behind his back: "Did you see that kid with no arm?" Naturally, his self-confidence was low. Only later in high school and college did he overcome such feelings. Even adults did not know how to treat him. Some would make a nice remark to him like, "Don't you have wonderful red hair," only to follow it with, "What happened to your arm?"

Over and over again, Kevin had to deal with looks and whispers. People would just stare at him. They generally looked at the face, then down to the arm, then up to the face. Kevin said, "Most of the time it is curiosity, but it can be extremely frustrating." He knew it was a mystery to children, but adults?

Kevin had to do something to improve the situation. What would you do? Kevin had to become strong. It helped that his parents had not coddled him since birth. They knew, too, that he would one day have to live on his own. Forget the easy Velcro tennis shoes that you did not have to tie! It was shoelaces for Kevin. Forget the easy, zippered pants when he was 2. Kevin had to learn to button them. Kevin ran with it. Even when he wanted to do a wheelie on his bike, and could not, and his mother got him a prosthetic arm so he could, Kevin would not use it. Because of his willingness to face his tasks with what he had, he went far in dealing with people and pursuing his dreams.

Soon he was playing sports with his dad. He loved basketball most, and his tall frame was suited for the game; but how do you play basketball with one arm? It was probably one of the hardest games he could have tried. Coaches would just look at him and say, "No. We do not want that kid on our team. He cannot help us win." Kevin then learned a secret about selling himself to others: work hard and prove to everyone you can do it. He practiced and practiced and practiced, but in seventh grade, he was cut from the middle school's team during trials. The coach told him that if he had had one spot left, Kevin would have gotten it.

Kevin was sad. Would you give up then? But Kevin was not a quitter. He knew he could play basketball. There had to be other teams! He went for the Amateur Athletic Union (AAU) where he had impressed Coach Patrick McKnight. It worked. People were beginning to see that Kevin was not just a kid without an arm, and that people with one arm were indeed capable of playing basketball.

But this was now, and Kevin had to fight for his victories. As people forgot his one arm, he learned he had another battle to face: the public's fascination with him.

By sophomore year, Kevin was on the high school team, and he was playing regularly: a little over 20 minutes per game, averaging 15 points, five blocks and six rebounds. He would jump up in the air at Amador Valley in Pleasanton, California, and dunk the basketball. Kevin would trap rebounds against his "Nub" and switch the ball quickly from it to the right hand to dribble and shoot. Oh, and now what fanfare! It was like the world had never seen anything so fantastic before! The media had awakened to his story. They were coming from everywhere scribbling in their notepads and flashing their lights with their cameras. Never had Kevin experienced such a hoopla!

Teammates bragged about him to reporters. They said Kevin's huge right hand amazed them, which incidentally compensated nicely for his bad left arm. One player described it as being as big as two hands. Others referred to it as a mitt and compared it to the net of a lacrosse stick. The impressed media would snap photos for their publications while the crowd rooted for Kevin. He could jump, steal the ball, and block like the best of them, and he was not a bad shooter either. He believed in himself and bigger things. His goal: play at Division I schools in college, at the highest level. He knew he was good enough, but would colleges think so? They would be tougher than these crowds.

Section I   The Athletes

In senior year, Kevin broke his leg. Now he knew the university teams would not select him. He was smart, however, and he decided to go to a military school in Virginia for post-graduate work to give him an edge at getting a scholarship at a university.

He was a top player at Fork Union Military School where he led the team in rebounding and blocked shots, but to his chagrin it did not matter to Division I schools. Kevin watched angrily as teammates got scholarships, whereas he struggled because college coaches were worried about their own careers and did not select him for their teams. "It was business," Kevin said. "I was doing the best I could and did not have a fair shot."

Division III and Division II schools lined up, but only three Division I schools considered him, and two could not find the money to pay him a scholarship. Finally, Manhattan College in New York City took the risk. The coach, Barry Rohrssen, said that coaches all the time take chances on kids that have behavior problems, poor academic histories, and injuries, many of whom did not appreciate the opportunity handed to them. Why not Kevin? He was not only inspiring for the rest of the team, but a good player. One time, after Kevin blocked 20 shots in one game, his teammates called him Laue Ming after the great, retired NBA Houston Rockets basketball player, Yao Ming. Kevin had become the first ever basketball player with one arm in Division I history!

At college, the media still clamored around him. His mentor, Jim Abbott, a famous Major League Baseball pitcher with one arm, told him to focus on the game when the cameras distracted him.

Kevin knows he will not be on a National Basketball Association (NBA) team. He does motivational speaking like Abbott now. Kevin has also accepted the attention he has received. He wants children who have one arm to have a role model.

Kevin does not lie on his bed sulking that he was born with a disability. His achievements, and the positive and negative attention he has received all his life, have formed his strong, compassionate, giving character. He would tell you to believe in yourself no matter what your imperfections, no matter what hurtful remarks others say to you; and then success, good relationships with people, and acceptance of yourself will come. If the media catches your story, and you are bombarded with attention, then accept it with grace and learn to deal with it. It is not easy, but worth it. In doing so, every day he is becoming a better master of his own fate.

If you had a like disability, do you think you could achieve your dream like he did? Kevin will be the first one to tell you "yes."

Section I The Athletes

Kevin Clinton Laue's Story

What do you think?

1. If you were Kevin, how would you deflect people's attention from your one arm? Would you do what he did?

2. Do you think it is natural for adults to be as curious as children when they see disabilities in others?

3. What type of disability have you seen? How did you react? After this story, would you react differently?

4. What do you think of Kevin refusing to use a prosthesis? Do you think he could have done more if he had used a prosthesis?

5. Do you think that more colleges will open the door to people with disabilities because of Kevin playing basketball at Manhattan?

6. Do you think the colleges and universities were right in closing their doors to Kevin because he had one arm, even though he did just as well as the others at military school?

7. What other sports do you think Kevin could play on a college or professional level?

8. Have you ever made fun of someone who has disabilities? Do you know of someone who has? What did they do or say? What would you say to them now?

Kevin Clinton Laue's Story

Did you know?

- Kevin Clinton Laue was born with one arm on April 13, 1990, in Pleasanton, California.
- After Kevin did not make his middle school's basketball team in seventh grade, he joined a traveling Amateur Athletic Union (AAU) basketball team, the Tri-Valley Outlawz, coached by Patrick McKnight. Kevin then earned himself the Defense Award and Inspirational Award.
- He attended Amador Valley High School in Pleasanton, California, where by his junior year he was considered a top player and a star and played about 23 minutes a game, averaging about 14 points, six blocks, and 12 rebounds.
- To realize his dream of playing for a Division I school, in 2008, he entered Fork Union Military Academy in Virginia for post-graduate education and to become better at basketball. Fletcher Arritt coached Kevin until Kevin left as part of the class of 2009. He averaged 10 points, 12 rebounds, and six blocks a game.
- In March 2009, Manhattan College gave him a scholarship. He majored in business with a 3.5 average while playing center on the basketball team. In 2010, he became the recipient of the Eastern College Athletic Conference (ECAC) Award of Valor given to student-athletes whose courage, motivation, and relentless determination serves as an inspiration to all.
- For the playing season at Manhattan for 2010-2011, Kevin made 22 appearances, starting in three contests: made first collegiate start at the 2010 Old Spice Classic against Georgia 11/28; scored a career-high six points; tied a career-high with two blocks and grabbed three rebounds over 14 minutes of action versus Binghamton 12/11; scored four points and pulled down a season-high five rebounds in a start at Bowling Green 12/22; scored four points in games against Hofstra 12/18, Loyola 1/7 Fairfield 1/28; scored

Section I   The Athletes

24 points, recorded 21 rebounds and blocked five shots during the season; and registered a .600 field goal percentage.

- He graduated from Manhattan in three years, and now travels the globe in Asia, Africa, and Europe, as a spokesperson for the Boys and Girls Club of New Jersey, inspiring others. He is on the board of the New Jersey Special Olympics. Through his speeches, his web site, www.kevinlaue.net, reads that "Today, Kevin challenges his audience to 'find their nub' and turn their own weaknesses in to a strength by understanding it better." You can find information on how to book him for speaking engagements on the web site.
- He is 6'11 inches and wears a size 17 shoe.
- Franklin Martin wrote the documentary film, *Long Shot: The Kevin Laue Story*. It played to excellent reviews. Cinipix, a new Hollywood studio, acquired it under the umbrella of financiers, Neil Grossman and Howard Silverman. In fall 2013, a major movie based on the documentary was released in several large American cities to rave reviews.

Nicholas Ryan Taylor
The Garage Door to Success

Photo courtesy of Nick Taylor

"You have to be willing to fail, but not willing to accept failure."

Nicholas Ryan Taylor's ball soared across the net at the U.S. Open. His opponent dashed for it, only to miss the slam. The crowd roared. Nick had scored, and coming up next would be the match point. Everyone was on their edge of their seats, quiet. Nick poised waiting for the serve. It came. He shot the ball into the far corner of the opposing court. Kaftovic had no hope of reaching it. The Men's Singles Championship trophy was Nick's! How grand it all was!

Section I   The Athletes

The alarm clock sounded. Nick awoke, his eyes gazing at his wheelchair. He sighed. The U.S. Open would not be for him. At his young age of 14, Nick did not know that the U.S. Open had a wheelchair division. Nick had a rare disability, *arthrogryposis*. *Arthrogryposis* is congenital, which means that he was born with it. The condition affected many of the motor nerves in his spine. Nick could not open his hands well. He had some movement in his legs, but could not walk. He had ridden in a power chair almost his whole life, which he drove with his right arm.

But Nick loved tennis. He loved it with a passion. It sang a special tune in his heart. He played tennis poorly, but "never give up" was his motto. Nick was tough. Maybe no one wanted to lob balls with him since he could only hit 10 feet in front of him, but that would not stop him. Instead, every day, while the other kids were bicycling in the street, he would pound the tennis ball against the garage door in hopes a person with no physical disabilities would play with him. He would forget about his medical condition, forget about any of his teenage problems and forget about his lack of ability. Little did he and his neighbors know that one day Nick would become a star, eventually hitting the ball 70 to 80 miles per hour. Now that was fast!

But for now the ball drummed, drummed, drummed against the wall. For two hours, he slammed the ball, his arm aching. Still he swung harder as he wheeled around in his power wheelchair, ignoring the setting sun and everyone going inside for dinner. The other kids were used to watching him practice late, even in the rain and snow; for Nick had decided he would keep at his drills and do well in this game even if he had to practice every night for years. One day, somebody would want to challenge him to a game on the courts. Any courts! He just knew it! He would fulfill his dream!

At last the moon rose high, and Nick put down his racket. He wiped his sweat off his brow with his towel. He had had enough. He went home, crashed in his bed and slept.

A school year came and went. Nick grew taller and stronger as a birthday went by. Things were looking up for him. His father had miraculously survived from the doctors' diagnosis of brain lesions, and Nick had gained a strong arm in playing tennis.

In high school, the tennis coach for the school invited him to play on the tennis team. Nick had found enough confidence in his game to say yes. Luckily, his wheelchair fit through the gate of the tennis court, unlike many courts in those days where the gates were not wide enough for wheelchairs. Back in 1995, most court operators did not want people to ride bicycles on courts, so they made the gates narrow. Wheelchairs could not roll through them. Fortunately for Nick, his high school's tennis court was not one of those courts.

From then on, Nick was on the high school team. He said, "I did horrible," but he still enjoyed it. During the four years of playing, he never won a singles match. He did win some doubles matches. As you can imagine, there were some days Nick went home, wanting to leave his racket in the closet after competing against other high school athletes. He would want to go back to his dream at the U.S. Open and stay there, but mostly the losses charged him with energy to do better. He said, "You have to be willing to fail, but not willing to accept failure." Because of this, Nick kept getting better.

As a freshman in high school, he had learned of wheelchair matches, and in 1995, he played in his first wheelchair tennis tournament. It was so much better to play against others like him. In the high school doubles matches, he had to make sure he did not run into his tennis partner having no physical disabilities with the wheelchair, which could hurt the person. At least here, he would be hitting another wheelchair. One safety precaution Nick always took was to wear his racket with a leather strap – like racquetball rackets – attached at the end of the handle. Nick would put the leather strap around his wrist and grip the tennis racket in his left hand, and that way it would not slip off and hit someone when he swung.

Section I The Athletes

How do you think Nick did in these matches? One day Nick was playing in an invitational against the number one wheelchair player in the world in the first round and won! He was so ecstatic that he wanted to spin his wheelchair around and around. To finally taste victory after years of hard work was like tasting the best pizza you have ever had and getting a trophy, too. Tears wanted to stream down his face. He was on his way.

More glory was to follow. The decisive moment in Nick's career was when he joined forces with David Wagner and played in doubles quad tournaments. They ended up winning many cups and then gold in three Paralympics – in Athens, Beijing and London. The duo was considered the number one wheelchair doubles quad team in the world. Nick had succeeded!

Nick is unusual with his tennis playing. He is the only tennis player in the world who serves by tossing the ball up with his foot. Nick's talent is not just due to his strong back. He said, "The important element of hitting the ball is turning the body into the ball and timing the contact with it at the right moment."

Want to make Nick's back bristle? Just tell him he cannot do something. It will only make him want to do it more. He will practice and practice until he will beat you. He is as competitive as Michael Phelps swimming for his eight golds at the Beijing Olympics. He lives for a challenge.

When he tells someone he plays tennis, Nick said, "People will say, 'Yeah right. There is no way you can play wheelchair tennis.'" He added, "I love the look on their faces when they find out I can…seeing that surprise. I enjoy creating that shock value. It knocks down the person's wrong perception of my disability. In the future when the person sees another person who has disabilities, he or she won't question their ability. But I'll do the same thing. I'll say they are just too disabled to play that sport. Then 10 to 15 seconds later I tell myself that I shouldn't make that assumption. That's the way others are looking at me!"

Nick encourages you to overcome your obstacles and grab your dream. What's your personal "garage door?" Go. Pound the ball against it. Win your gold medal while knocking down someone else's wrong assumptions about you.

Section I The Athletes

Nicholas Ryan Taylor's Story
What do you think?

1. Do you think you would have the perseverance and determination to keep on practicing a sport, as Nick did in his story?

2. Do you think after some practice, you could serve a tennis ball with your foot?

3. Does this story give you some ideas about where you can practice your sport other than the gym?

4. Does this story inspire you to not give up on your dreams?

5. What does "What is your garage door" mean?

6. What is your dream? How do you intend to fulfill it?

7. How have other athletes overcome their disabilities and fulfilled their dream?

8. If you had a disability, how would you participate in a sport? Would you quit? What would keep you going if you did not?

Nicholas Ryan Taylor's Story

Did you know?

- Nick was born on November 12, 1979, in Wichita, Kansas.
- According to The International Tennis Federation, as of November 18, 2013, Nick and David Wagner were the number one men's quad doubles team in the world. They are known as the most successful wheelchair duo in history. In 2013, Nick was considered to be the number four men's singles quad player wheelchair player in the world. To be eligible for the quad division, an athlete has to have three limbs that are disabled.
- He has won over 200 career titles in various wheelchair divisions.
- Nick and David Wagner won gold medals in the 2004 Athens, Greece, the 2008 Beijing, China, and the 2012 London, England, Paralympics quad doubles wheelchair tennis. They also have earned six U.S. Open titles and four Australian Open Titles. Nick won bronze in the men's quad singles in wheelchair tennis at the 2012 London, England, Paralympics. He has spent a decade in the top five of singles championships. In 2013, he was a 10-time grand slam winner.
- The U.S. Olympic Committee named David and Nick "Paralympic Team of the Year" for 2012.
- Nick was voted the 1999 United States Tennis Association (USTA) Player of the Year and has been on the United States National Team for the World Team Cup since 2000. The Tennis Industry magazine released in January 2014 that Nick was their Wheelchair Tennis Champion of the Year.
- Nick earned himself a Masters of Sports Administration from Wichita State University in 2007. He is now the Volunteer Director of Operations

Section I The Athletes

for the Wichita State University men's tennis team after serving as the men and women's team manager for four years.
- Nick is vice president of the Wichita-based, Wheelchair Sports, Inc.
- He serves as chair of the Missouri Valley section of Diversity and Inclusion Committee and does motivational speaking.

Jessica Tatiana Long
Slicing Through the Water with Humor

Photo courtesy of Jessica Long

"I want anyone with a disability to be able to say, 'If she can do that, I can do something else.'"

Sixteen-year-old gold medal-winning Paralympic swimmer, Jessica Tatiana Long, was up to no good this afternoon at the shore. She was a girl with two legs below the knees amputated and had some mischievous plans. She looked around and when she saw no one was looking, she stuck her natural-looking prosthetic legs (artificial

Section I The Athletes

legs) in the sand with the bottom of the feet pointing up to the sky and slipped away into the ocean and waited. She giggled under her breath. She could not wait to watch people's reaction at thinking someone was buried head first on the beach as they walked by. Jessica was a devilish one! Soon along came someone, and boy did he do a double take. "Huh?" Jessica heard him mumble. She cracked up laughing in the sea. Having prostheses could be so much fun if you just knew how to use them! Jessica enjoyed creating humorous situations with her disability rather than having others take it so seriously and stare at her with no limbs below her knees. She had experienced that plenty of times in her young life! And that was definitely no fun!

She was born in an orphanage in Siberia with several bones missing in her lower legs and feet. Eighteen months after she came to America, having been adopted by Steve and Beth Long, she had had surgery to have her legs below her knees amputated. The orphanage was a gloomy place with broken windows and not enough cribs for the babies, but it had not dampened Jessica's spirits.

It helped that the Longs whisked her away to America when she was just a little thing, but on U.S. soil, others were always looking at her because of her amputation. Can you imagine what it would be like to be minding your own business in a store, only to experience some parents pointing at you and tapping their kids on the shoulders, to show them your amputated legs? And to make matters worse, whispering to their kids about you like you did not exist or hear them, only you did? In fact, you heard every word! It would be awful! You might get bitter, want to hide, or even yell at them to stop! Jessica did none of the above. Yet the adults annoyed her. They should have known better and shown respect toward her. Kids were different, she thought. It was natural for kids to be curious and ask questions. She actually did not mind. She knew they did not understand the problem. In the end, the comments of the adults made her more self-conscious during the summers. She would wear long pants to cover up her prostheses.

It was not until she was 12 years old, when she became the youngest member of the Paralympics elite swim team that she noticed that these great athletes shrugged off people's rude behavior toward them. Their attitude helped Jessica change. Instead, if someone was pointing at her again, she would think, "Seriously, is this really happening? I'm a bigger person than this," and she would walk away. Friends would even say out loud, "She doesn't have any legs" in front of the ill-mannered adults, in order to say, "We know you are staring." If Jessica did get flustered in these situations, it would only make her work harder and not give up, and Jessica was a tough competitor already.

The whole experience of dealing with this behavior from some members of the public helped Jessica to develop a wicked sense of humor about her disability, because she knew that if she took her disability less seriously, maybe they would too, and their comments would not bother her. Humor has a wonderful way of dulling the edge of a sharp piece of glass. Jessica liked to have fun, too. Once when a reporter came from *The Washington Post* to do a story on her at her pool, Jessica decided to get him and others to think it hurt to walk on her knees, when it did not. She walked on them down the side of the pool, going, "Ouch, ouch, ouch."

Another time, when she was 16, she went to a salon with her friends who were having pedicures. Jessica pulled up her pant legs to show her naturally made prostheses to the pedicurist with the already painted toenails on them. The lady did not know what to do. She was confused. Jessica then told her that the legs were artificial, and they both laughed.

Jessica has found life with prostheses can be funny even when she least expects it. At the age of 13, she went skiing at Massanutten, Virginia. She did not want to go on the ski lift because she was afraid that when the lift jolted forward, her prostheses would fall off. They were not as well-made back then, as they were not locked in with a pin. Her sister assured her that she would ask the operator of the ski lift to slow the lift down, but it climbed as usual. Jessica sat on the lift. It went

Section I The Athletes

up and her prostheses came off. The jaws dropped of the people in the lines behind her. It became even funnier when the skiers saw the two prostheses going up later by themselves.

Soon after when Jessica went ice-skating and fell, the legs came off again and this time shot across the ice. Jessica's face turned red. A kind person brought the prostheses back. Today, she laughs about the two incidents. She realized life and sports with a disability has its hilarious moments. Just bring along your sense of humor to enjoy the amusing times, as she does. Then the walls between you and those who do not understand will come crumbling down. It is one reason she is a gold medalist Paralympic swimmer. She can see light where others see darkness and can create sunshine wherever she goes. There is no barrier to others when you can laugh at yourself.

Opening the Gate

Jessica Tatiana Long's Story

What do you think?

1. If you had a disability, would you be able to laugh at yourself?

2. Do you think it was right how people treated Jessica when they saw her amputated legs?

3. Do you admire Jessica for her humor?

4. Did you think some of the jokes that Jessica played on others were funny? Why? Or why not?

5. How would you deal with others if they pointed at you with a disability?

6. Are you able to laugh at yourself even if you do not have a disability?

7. How does humor have the ability to knock down barriers between people?

Section I The Athletes

Jessica Tatiana Long's Story
Did you know?

- Jessica Long was born Tatiana Olegovna Kirollova on February 29, 1992, with fibular hemimelia. She did not have fibulas, ankles, and heels and most of the other bones in her feet.
- Steve and Beth Long of Maryland adopted her from a grim orphanage in Siberia when she was 13 months old and took her to America to live. She has five other siblings.
- She learned to swim in her grandparents' pool where she and her sisters would spend hours pretending they were mermaids.
- She joined her first competitive team at age 10 and now holds more than 12 Paralympic records, world records, and medals of all colors from various world events.
- Jessica has been on the elite Paralympics swim team since 2004. In her first meet at age 12, she won three gold medals.
- In 2006, she was named the U.S. Olympic Committee's Paralympian of the Year.
- In 2007 and 2013, she was the recipient of the ESPN Best Female Athlete with a Disability ESPY (Excellence in Sports Performance Yearly Award).
- In 2007, she was the first Paralympic athlete to win the Amateur Athletic Union (AAU) James E. Sullivan Award honoring her as the best amateur athlete in the United States. It is her most cherished award because it does not focus on her disability but rather her athleticism.
- Also in 2007, Jessica was selected as USA Swimming's Disability Swimmer of the Year (the Trisha L. Zorn Award).
- In 2008, she was the recipient of the Juan Antonio Samaranch IOC Disabled Athlete Award.

- In 2006 and 2011, she was named the Disabled Swimmer of the Year by *Swimming World* magazine.
- On February 18, 2014, during the Sochi Olympics, NBC released a documentary on Jessica Long's journey to her birth family in the Irkutsk region of Siberia. The documentary was called, *Long Way Home: The Jessica Long Story*. Jessica met her birth parents. They were teenagers when they gave her up for adoption and could not care for her because of her disability. She saw her three siblings, as well.
- She has won numerous events in the Athens Paralympics, at Beijing and London, and is currently training at Loyola University in Baltimore, Maryland under coach, Brian Loeffler, for the 2016 Rio de Janeiro, Paralympics.
- She has participated in gymnastics, basketball, cheerleading, ice skating, biking, running, and rock climbing. Her hobbies include yoga, Pilates, interior decorating, reading, and traveling.
- Jessica's biggest role model and inspiration is Erin Popovich. Her favorite movie is *A Walk to Remember*. She loves Chinese food, Jesus, coffee, old bookstores, and yoga pants. The elephant is her favorite animal.
- Her favorite quote is by Christopher Robin: "Promise me you'll always remember: you're braver than you believe, and stronger than you seem, and smarter than you think."
- She is now 23 years old.

Section I   The Athletes

Opening the Gate

Hannah Vjollca McFadden
Train with the Heart of a Diamond

Photo courtesy of Deborah McFadden

"Find a coach who believes in you. Don't find one who is negative."
"If you try one way, and it doesn't work; try another way."

Sweat matted Hannah Vjollca McFadden's hair. Her shirt was damp. Up in the air she lifted heavy weights. She only rested for a moment as necessary. Everyone in the gym saw that she trained harder than anyone else. No one wanted to cross paths with her in wheelchair track and field. She was a force to be reckoned with in her sport. You could see her muscles.

Hannah had long understood how important training was in an athletic career. From her time as a little one in an orphanage in Albania, Hannah knew she had to work hard to keep in line with the others like the Energizer bunny who kept going and going. For Hannah was born not having a femur (thigh bone) or a left hip. She suffered from a medical condition called proximal femoral focal deficiency, which as she grew would require her to walk with an artificial leg, called a prosthesis. But in the orphanage, she did not have one. It did not stop her.

From the minute she could crawl, she raced to the dinner table in order to reach it first. At age 3½, she would hop on one leg or use crutches. Nothing deterred Hannah. Not then, not later. At a young age, she was already training herself to face the grueling mental and physical challenges of sport. You can train, too. You must train to achieve greatness in an athletic career.

Deborah McFadden, president of the International Children's Alliance in Maryland, adopted Hannah. Deborah saw a tough spirit in Hannah. She encouraged it in the United States. Unlike some parents, she did not baby Hannah. She said, "A number of elite athletes are adopted. Every parent should say to a child, 'How can I help you be the best you can be?'" Once when Hannah fell down in a mall, Deborah said, "Good fall, Hannah!" Even though she felt all choked up inside, she did not come to the rescue. A lady came over to Deborah upset and said, "Aren't you going to help her?" Deborah responded, "I am helping her. It is part of her training. It may be hard to see a child struggle, but it will help her do something else."

Hannah said, "My mother not coddling me taught me not to give up and not need people to help me. I can take a harder workout, subsequently." Hannah now never gives up. One time at school when the children were rope climbing, many of them could not figure out how to do it. The staff was especially wondering about Hannah. They asked her mother if Hannah would be okay. Deborah saw that many of the kids were afraid. One was crying. Teachers were holding their breath, but Hannah shimmied up the rope with one leg. She thought she could do it and just figured out how. Hannah showed them that mental attitude is crucial. Do you think of different ways to do a task? Even with humor?

Hannah did not like others to focus on her disability. She did not want to focus on it either. One day, at age 7, kids were asking so many questions about her condition that finally fed up, she said to one child, "I just didn't drink enough milk." To this day, her mom wonders if there is a child out there who is afraid not to drink his milk.

It helped that Deborah talked to the first and second graders about Hannah's disability because then the kids did not care that she was so different than them. They would ask instead of Hannah, "What can you do with your disability?" The children would tell Deborah that Hannah was the best "hopper" in class. Deborah said, "When you are comfortable with your disability, others are too."

Hannah was definitely comfortable. One day when her sixth grade class went rope climbing, Hannah's prosthesis fell to the ground. Hannah thought, "Oh, well," but the teacher panicked. Hannah found it funny. "I fell in school all the time. I laughed at myself. Friends would say, 'Oh, Hannah, always falling.' They would laugh at me, too. Being embarrassed won't help you. So it doesn't affect my training. I would fall a lot during walking and training and just go on and pretend like nothing happened."

Her sense of humor and fun in life kept her mentally loose when she was not training in high school. She liked to pick out fabrics and designs for her prostheses. She had pink and purple sparkling ones. Her mother said then that when she was older, she could have skin-colored ones. Hannah was not interested.

At Halloween, her whimsical spirit comes out. One October, her artificial foot felt loose and fell off. Hannah got the idea to become a legless pirate for Halloween. She

Section I   The Athletes

put a parrot on her shoulder and took the foot off her prosthesis. Hannah then walked around and said, "Aye" to everyone's amusement.

Her humor and her tough mental mindset all help Hannah with the arduous physical training she must go through to perform well in her sports. When Hannah is doing ambulatory sports (sports done on legs), her body functions with all the force on one leg. Her hopping in the orphanage strengthened the key muscles at a young age, but still she must train them to make her leg strong. She has to use all her muscles; whereas, an athlete with no physical disabilities does not. Hannah said, "My body gets sorer than theirs. I need to do squats on one leg. Balancing on it can be hard." She works a lot more on strength training of the arms because she uses them more. She said, "Basically I use the same drills as an able-bodied athlete. People will say, 'You are so lucky you are so good.' I say, 'No I work at it.' It becomes easier as I do it because I'm used to it. But I still work harder because I want it to be a challenge."

The hard physical training helps Hannah recover quicker from injuries. It could even save her life. Hannah's older sister, Tatyana, who also has a disability, and is an accomplished Paralympics medal-winning wheelchair racer and Nordic skier, was once told by her doctors that probably the only reason she survived a medical problem was because of her training and her fitness.

Hannah said that all athletes, those without physical disabilities and those with disabilities, have similar aspects to their training. This includes, from the start, learning the intellectual components: knowing the rules of the sport, its foundation and the requirements of the coach. It is important before hard-core training to take smaller steps first. Take two days of rest. Eat right, stay dehydrated and sleep well.

Hannah said, "As I get older, training is harder. It is more of an intellectual challenge, learning how to train better, what to do and what not to do. Finding the right coach is everything." Hannah said, "My coaches believe in me." She stressed and added, "Don't find one that is negative."

Training is more than sprints. Training is more than push-ups. It is more than drills. Hannah will tell you that it is the key to success at any sport. Just remember that Hannah believes in "no train, no gain." It is why at the age of 16, she went to the Paralympics in London for summer 2012 and was the youngest member on the team to compete against her sister in the 100-meter T54 wheelchair race. She placed eighth.

If there is a time you feel training has just gotten too tough, then think of Hannah shimmying up the rope on her one leg, the athlete with the heart of a diamond. It might give you the extra energy and will to say, "I can do this. I will keep training."

Section I   The Athletes

Hannah Vjollca McFadden's Story

What do you think?

1. Do you think Hannah had a lot of courage in facing her disability? How do you think she got this courage?

2. Does Hannah inspire you to attempt a physical feat within limits of safety that you would not have achieved before?

3. Did Hannah's story make you more comfortable about her prosthesis?

4. Now that you have read Hannah's story, would you think twice about asking too many questions about a person's disability? How could you find another way to learn about it?

5. What do you think drives Hannah to train so hard?

6. What did you learn from the story about the important aspects of training?

7. Did you think Hannah's mother, Deborah McFadden, played any role in making Hannah grow up as strong as she is?

8. What was your favorite part of the story?

Hannah Vjollca McFadden's Story

Did you know?

- Hannah Vjollca McFadden was born on January 23, 1996, in Duress, Albania, with a rare disability called proximal femoral focal deficiency (PFFD). She had no left hip or femur.
- Deborah McFadden, president of the International Children's Alliance in Maryland, adopted her at age 3½ years old.
- In August 2010, at the Olomouc Czechoslovakia International Wheelchair and Ambulatory Sport (IWAS) Junior World Games for ages under 23, Hannah won six silver medals: three for track and field for the 100m, 200m and 400m; two for swimming for the 50m and freestyle; and one for field in shot put. She races in a specially designed wheelchair and uses a specially designed chair for field events.
- She holds the U.S. Junior National Disability Championship Ambulatory Table Tennis title for 2010 in her class. The class of an athlete with disabilities is determined by which ones of his/her muscles function.
- In 2011 and 2012, Hannah joined the All-American High School Track and Field Team.
- She participated in the T54 category of the 100m-wheelchair race against her sister, Tatyana McFadden, in the 2012 London Paralympics. She came in third in the U.S. trials while her sister came in first. The "T" in "T54" stands for "track" and the "54" number indicates that they are wheelchair athletes with various levels of spinal cord injuries and amputations. Hannah, at 16 years old, was the youngest member of the U.S. team. Tatyana and Hannah were the first siblings in history to compete together in the Paralympics. In London, she placed eighth.

Section I The Athletes

- Hannah plays three main sports: wheelchair basketball, swimming, and track and field. Her hobbies are scuba diving, downhill skiing, and ice hockey. She is an excellent lacrosse player. She enjoys cooking.
- She attended Atholton High School in Clarksville, Maryland, where she was on the Honor Roll, and now attends University of Illinois at Urbana-Champaign as a sophomore because of its strong wheelchair basketball program, wheelchair track and field program, and academic program. She is majoring in international business.
- She was named the U.S. Paralympics Track and Field High School All-American for the years, 2012 and 2013.
- In October 2013, Hannah made the USOC National Paralympic Team.
- In June 2015, at the U.S. Paralympics Track and Field Nationals, she won gold in the 200m T-54 wheelchair race, and three silvers in the 100m, the 400m and the 800m.
- She has been selected for the 2015 U.S. National Paralympic Track and Field team, and plans to go to the world championships in the fall and Rio de Janeiro for the World Paralympics in 2016.

Greg Gontaryk
The Tech Talk of a Baseball

Photo of Greg Gontaryk courtesy of Robert Memory.

Hot dogs! Anyone? Hot dogs! Popcorn for sale! Popcorn for sale! A camera flashes. The fan's hair is streaked with yellow and green dye, and his face is painted. He is screaming, "Slam that ball, Henry!" Dirt smudges the uniform of a baseball player as he slides into third base. The hometown crowd suddenly jumps to its feet and roars as its favorite star blasts one over the fence. Excitement ripples through the stadium as the scoreboard racks up two more runs against the visitors. It is an evening at the old ball game.

Section I   The Athletes

No one ever comes to watch just the game. Fans come for the smells, the taste, the touch, the sounds, and the sight of it. But what if you cannot see? What if you were literally "in the dark" at the stadium and were asked to play? What would you do?

In such a situation, you could probably imagine being hit in the head with the baseball when trying to bat, or running toward the stands instead of a base, or never catching the ball, and you would probably be right.

But stop…What if you were visually impaired and someone made it possible for you to play. Wouldn't that be thrilling?

In the early 1960s and '70s, inventors asked the question, "What if those who were visually impaired could play baseball?" and made it possible. The Telephone Pioneers of America Volunteers, now called just the Pioneers, crafted a ball that beeped - the beep baseball - which athletes who had visual impairments could field. Not only did the Pioneers invent a beeping ball, but they also designed 4-foot-tall vinyl-covered towers to set up as bases with speakers inside that transmitted a buzz for the athletes who were visually impaired to hear as they ran toward them. The Pioneers thought of everything!

I bet you are wondering how this game is played? Is it the same as the baseball of the St. Louis Cardinals and the Milwaukee Brewers, two professional teams in Major League Baseball? Well, no, not exactly. For you see, there are only two bases in beep baseball, one at first and one at third, and the hitter with visually impairments only runs to one to score. I know that sounds a bit odd to you, since you are used to a baseball player running around four bases; but the athlete who cannot see well would most likely collide with the fielders if he did that!

Want to know how to play it? Take a moment and close your eyes. Imagine yourself on a grassy field. You are standing next to home plate. No one is making a noise. It is so quiet you can hear your heart beat. Bob Memory, a volunteer who is visually impaired, and is on a team in Philadelphia, Pennsylvania, called the Wolfpack, said,

Greg Gontaryk
The Tech Talk of a Baseball

Photo of Greg Gontaryk courtesy of Robert Memory.

Hot dogs! Anyone? Hot dogs! Popcorn for sale! Popcorn for sale! A camera flashes. The fan's hair is streaked with yellow and green dye, and his face is painted. He is screaming, "Slam that ball, Henry!" Dirt smudges the uniform of a baseball player as he slides into third base. The hometown crowd suddenly jumps to its feet and roars as its favorite star blasts one over the fence. Excitement ripples through the stadium as the scoreboard racks up two more runs against the visitors. It is an evening at the old ball game.

Section I   The Athletes

No one ever comes to watch just the game. Fans come for the smells, the taste, the touch, the sounds, and the sight of it. But what if you cannot see? What if you were literally "in the dark" at the stadium and were asked to play? What would you do?

In such a situation, you could probably imagine being hit in the head with the baseball when trying to bat, or running toward the stands instead of a base, or never catching the ball, and you would probably be right.

But stop...What if you were visually impaired and someone made it possible for you to play. Wouldn't that be thrilling?

In the early 1960s and '70s, inventors asked the question, "What if those who were visually impaired could play baseball?" and made it possible. The Telephone Pioneers of America Volunteers, now called just the Pioneers, crafted a ball that beeped - the beep baseball - which athletes who had visual impairments could field. Not only did the Pioneers invent a beeping ball, but they also designed 4-foot-tall vinyl-covered towers to set up as bases with speakers inside that transmitted a buzz for the athletes who were visually impaired to hear as they ran toward them. The Pioneers thought of everything!

I bet you are wondering how this game is played? Is it the same as the baseball of the St. Louis Cardinals and the Milwaukee Brewers, two professional teams in Major League Baseball? Well, no, not exactly. For you see, there are only two bases in beep baseball, one at first and one at third, and the hitter with visually impairments only runs to one to score. I know that sounds a bit odd to you, since you are used to a baseball player running around four bases; but the athlete who cannot see well would most likely collide with the fielders if he did that!

Want to know how to play it? Take a moment and close your eyes. Imagine yourself on a grassy field. You are standing next to home plate. No one is making a noise. It is so quiet you can hear your heart beat. Bob Memory, a volunteer who is visually impaired, and is on a team in Philadelphia, Pennsylvania, called the Wolfpack, said,

Opening the Gate

"Beep baseball is the quietest game on earth because everything is hearing sensitive." For you see, the athletes who have visual impairments must be able to hear the beeping ball and the buzzing towers.

You listen. You hear the athletes hurrying to their designated zones in the field ready to get you out. All of them are wearing a blindfold to give them an equal chance at the ball since some of the players have more sight than others.

Now it is time for you to pick up the bat. You know you will swing at everything because you cannot see a perfect pitch with your closed eyes; but the pitcher and catcher, who both have sight, are working with you to hit the ball. What? You say. Why would they want to do that? Are they not on the opposing team, like in regular baseball? No, not in beep baseball. They are on your team. It is their job to help you, and they are your eyes! Imagine if you had visual impairments and had to try to figure out what type of pitch was heading toward you. Your head would swirl! No, the pitcher must know how to lob the ball to you straight over the plate each time at the same speed. He and the catcher are your teammates.

They have worked with you for months, assisted by the baseball coach to help you not chop the ball, or slice the air, or loop the bat, all of which are easy to do when you cannot see. You have learned to know the pitcher's toss. Now is your time to show your stuff. Stillness marks the field. Not even a whisper in the air. Everyone is hushed.

The catcher yells, "Set" in a big booming voice to alert everyone he is prepared to receive the pitch. The pitcher replies, "Ready" and then he cries, "Pitch." Immediately, zooming toward you from 20 feet is a beeping noise, louder and louder. It is the baseball! But the beeping is not for you. It is for the fielders who are all now listening closely to know when the ball will come out to them in the grass. You block out the sound. Timing of the swing is the key. You count to yourself. One, two, three. Now! Swing! Slam goes the bat against the ball! Pound, Pound goes your heart.

Section I   The Athletes

Beep Baseball image courtesy of John Lykowski.

Out in the field the ball soars. Off in the distance, 100 feet away, you hear the buzzing noise of the vinyl-padded tower, which a volunteer, the base operator, has switched on randomly from the possible two bases. You run toward it as fast as a horse galloping in the woods, carrying a rider with an urgent message. As you race toward the base, you are careful. You have heard of a time when a batter ran to the non-buzzing base or even up the middle of the field!

Meanwhile out in the field, one of the two spotters (volunteers who are sighted) calls the number of the zone of a fielder where the ball is about to drop. The fielder now knows the ball is headed straight for him and is "fair," meaning it has traveled a minimum of 40 feet. The fielder searches for the ball in the grass with his fingers outstretched like a big spider's legs, feeling the blades between them. Rarely would the fielder catch the ball, but what an achievement that would be! Soon he raises the ball to the sky, shouting, "Up," excitedly telling all that he has it, but is it in time? Have you reached the base before his triumph? Are you out with his "Up"?

No, you have already charged into the tower and tumbled past it to the ground. You have scored a run for your team. Your team knows it and is cheering.

Members of the Philadelphia Wolfpack hold you as one of their best players. Yesterday, you hit a home run and earned the team two points by hitting the ball 170 feet, and then making it to the buzzing base in the required 30 seconds.

The fielder rolls the ball to the pitcher, and once again a batter strides to home plate for his turn to score for his team. You open your eyes. That was thrilling! Beep baseball has many different rules from regular baseball, but to those who are visually impaired, it is just as fun as regular baseball and even rougher.

Greg Gontaryk is an athlete who has visual impairments that is the manager of the Philadelphia Wolfpack Beep Baseball Team at Naylors Run Park in Upper Darby, Pennsylvania. He has played the game since 1983. He suffers from a hereditary medical condition called *retinoblastoma*, which is a form of eye cancer. He lost one eye at age 2, the other at age 3.

He said that "beep baseball can be a dangerous game" because major injuries do occur, such as broken legs, arms, and shoulders from a base runner colliding into a fielder, but this happens rarely. The sighted spotters and umpires warn against such collisions.

Greg said, "Older players wear elbow, hip, and knee pads as protection because of the diving on the ground. Younger ones are injured more because they do not want to wear the gear. They think they are all too good."

You do not have to be a player to be injured. Greg said one of their guys hit something with the ball every time he was up to bat. "It was just automatic. In one game he hit a car, a lady in a wheelchair, and a seeing-eye dog. We called him, 'The Assassin.'"

The game of beep baseball requires toughness. Stephen Guerra, Secretary of the National Beep Baseball Association (NBBA), said that individuals who want special treatment do not belong in beep baseball. The game needs volunteers that are

Section I The Athletes

sighted "who are not afraid to tell a person who is blind to get their duff in gear and get with the program if necessary. The blind do not need pampering," he said.

Many individuals who are legally visually impaired want to play baseball because it is an All-American sport, but the country lacks many teams because of the time needed to practice; and there are few sighted pitchers, catchers, and umpires interested in participating. Perhaps one day you will want to become one and help to spread the sport.

In the 1980s, the sport had approximately 25 teams; but now in 2015, they have 35, including one from Canada and another from Taiwan. All the regions in the U.S. are represented. The NBBA tried to get other countries to join in the action, but only Taiwan and Canada formed a team. Taiwan won several of the World Series, which usually begins in August.

Different ages play beep baseball, from teenagers to senior citizens. The sport is not in the Paralympics yet. Because the teams do not sell tickets to the events, they have to hold fundraisers to make their money. Still, even when the teams are ready to compete, it only takes one key person to back out and ruin an event for all. Greg said, "One time, all the players for both teams were set until a pitcher decided not to go." Can you imagine what a disappointment he caused for everyone else? The game was cancelled. Everyone had to scramble to get his or her money returned from the airline.

The Telephone Pioneers of America made the game of beep baseball possible for those with visually impairments with its technological design of the baseball, but players would still like a way to improve the ball. Perhaps it will be you who will give them the new design. Go read the NBBA rules off its website, www.nbba.org, and attend some games. You could electrify a sport.

Opening the Gate

Greg Gontaryk's Story

What do you think?

1. Do you think those who are visually impaired should try to play baseball, even with a beeping ball and a buzzing base?

2. What did you think of the invention of the Pioneers?

3. Do you think you could invent some way for an athlete with a disability to pursue a sport?

4. Do you know of any other ways that technology has helped athletes with disabilities?

5. Would you like to see beep baseball grow as a sport?

6. Do you think it would be hard to be quiet during the play of beep baseball, to allow the athletes to hear? Do you think this would be a fun game to watch? Would it be difficult not to talk during the game?

7. Now that you see that beep baseball needs volunteers, when you are older would you consider volunteering for those who have visually impairments, so they can play this American sport?

8. What do you think of the game of beep baseball?

Section I   The Athletes

Greg Gontaryk's Story

Did you know?

- Greg Gontaryk was born on June 8, 1951, in New York, New York.
- He suffers from a hereditary disease called *retinoblastoma,* a form of cancer, losing one eye at the age of 2, the other at the age of 3.
- He started playing beep baseball with the Philadelphia Warriors in 1983 till 1988, and has participated on other teams since then in Oklahoma, Texas, Kansas, Ohio, and California. He is now manager of the Philadelphia Wolfpack Beep Baseball Team at Naylors Run Park in Upper Darby, Pennsylvania.
- He played with all the teams in the World Series and other tournaments when his current hometown team could not go.
- Greg has won many awards from the NBBA, including Most Valuable Player for Defense, plus many all-tournament defense awards.
- On the field, he wears an old-fashioned, baseball uniform.
- In college, he rode stroke in crew. Previously, he bowled.
- He loves to participate in goalball, another sport for those who are visually impaired, which is included in the Paralympics. His team, the Pennsylvania Tornado, won many national championships and regional gold medals. From 1999 to 2010, his goalball team won six national championships.
- More information about the National Beep Baseball Association can be found at www.nbba.org.

Anthony Netto
A Hole-in-One with Disabilities in Sports

Photo courtesy of Anthony Netto.

"It's the ability, not the disability, which makes a good golfer."

"Everyone has a disability in golf, even if not physical."

"Learning to hit the ball far or into the hole…that's what it is about and not learning about your missing arm, or leg, or aches, or pains."

"What is that man doing strapped in front of that golf cart?" asked Todd of his father. Todd looked down the golf course perplexed, as he saw a large man with straps around his waist and leg braces around his knees in a vehicle that had the man standing against a frame. His feet were on a footrest in a three-wheeled, teardrop-shaped cart.

Section I   The Athletes

"Why, I think he is playing golf," his father replied, "How odd."

"Do you suppose he would mind if we asked him about it?" Todd said, still staring at the man.

"I think we'd better not bother him," Todd's father said.

The man was Anthony Netto. If he had known Todd and his dad wanted to speak to him, he would have let them ask him all the questions they wanted about the contraption. For you see, Anthony was no ordinary golfer, and the golf cart was no ordinary vehicle. Anthony was an individual with disabilities, incompletely paralyzed below the waist, and the cart was a stand-up-and-play wheelchair used on some golf courses called a Paramobile or Paragolfer. With the help of his golfer friend, Christian Nachtwey, and other engineers, Anthony had developed its rough design in 2001. The Paramobile is just one more way those with disabilities are crossing barriers in sports previously unavailable to them.

Now you – being young – would probably like to scoot around on it, as if it were a toy car, but for a person with disabilities, like Anthony, the Paramobile is much more than a play thing. Do you want to hear about Anthony and his creation? Then listen, and you will learn how all things are possible when you open a door.

Anthony learned to play golf in South Africa when he was 5 years old. After many years of swinging the club, he became a golf pro. Perhaps he could have become another Phil Mickelson, but that story was not to be.

Unfortunately, Anthony was injured in a war and by an accident with a drunk driver, leaving him incompletely paralyzed from the waist down and leaving his hands numb and unable to function well. You thought your life was rough! Anthony was devastated. Wouldn't you be? All your life you could walk, play your favorite sport, and suddenly, in a matter of years, bad luck disables your body. Anthony was sad, angry, frustrated, and in despair. He was tied up in knots.

Fortunately, the medical profession knew how he felt. They had dealt with others who had been paralyzed. There were kids with him in rehabilitation at the hospital and those smart, caring physical therapists egged them on to ask Anthony for golf lessons, getting him to promise he would teach them. They affectionately called him, "Flipper," because of his floppy working hands. What was Anthony to do? He, too, wanted to get back to golf. He loved it so.

One boy especially affected him: a 14 year old, who at 9 months old had become paralyzed because his mother's car had rolled during an accident when he was in the car seat in the back. He had gone through painful operation after operation, but with his drooling smile, he had a cocky attitude that told Anthony he had better wake up and realize life was not over when one becomes disabled. He could make life good for himself if he was willing to work hard. A window suddenly opened for Anthony.

Anthony knew then that he needed to get back on the golf course, but the golf carts available for golfers with disabilities, called Riders, did not excite him. He did not want to sit down playing golf. No, that was not for him. How could you hit your best shot that way? Often, one had to swing the club with one hand. Besides, sitting too long in wheelchair-type vehicles came with some dangerous problems. They caused pressure sores to develop, and if they got infected, well, that was bad news. They could tear the skin. You did not get good exercise sitting down either. Muscles and bones would gradually weaken over time if they were not being used. No, Anthony had been a golf pro in South Africa. He had always aimed high and asked for the best. Playing golf disabled would be no different.

Off to Germany went Anthony. For 12 years, he and his friend, Christian, and a group of talented engineers hacked away at ideas on how to improve the golf cart wheelchair to allow the golfer with disabilities to stand up and play. Finally, in 2001, the Paramobile was built. By 2011, over 20 countries were using this

Section I   The Athletes

product, of which 70 of the golf carts were in America. Now, in 2015, there are approximately 500 Paramobiles in the world in 22 countries with most in America. In the United States, there are 170, with every week more being ordered. Veterans use 85 percent of them with the support of funding by the veterans' organizations. This now includes Vietnam veterans. Recently, the wife of a veteran called him to tell him how thrilled her husband was now that the Paramobile allowed him to play golf better again. He had loved the game, too.

The teardrop-shaped vehicle is operated by a joystick and has a rechargeable battery that can make the cart run for more than 18 holes. Anthony is strapped in with a belt at his knees, one at his waist, and another large strap at the breast against a frame. From using the Paramobile, Anthony has developed so much core strength from standing up that he now can swing with two hands. To zip around the golf course, he sits down in the front, and then when he is ready to play, a hydraulic lift places him in a standing position with his feet resting on a platform. You can use it, too, but you have to be at least 3 feet, 2 inches tall. The backrest, standing frame, and footrest are adjustable.

Anthony was so excited with how well the vehicle worked; it was better than he had ever imagined. Since he has started using it, he has regained his function in his hands; his core muscles are stronger; and he is more mobile in his joints - all because of the exercise he now gets on the golf course from sitting up and down and standing. Not only that, he can breathe and digest his food better and his blood circulates to a 'T'. But best of all, it helps him with shooting the golf ball straighter and further than he could with the single Rider golf cart. Now that is awesome! All because he dreamed big things!

He just feels better. He does not have to look up at all the golfers around him either, who did not make him feel good about himself. He can look them straight in the eye.

How would you like to be way down below while everyone is talking above you about his/her golf shots?

His game of golf came back. In fact, in a charity shootout in Hamburg, Germany, a couple of years ago, he played a one-shot game against pros, such as Tiger Woods. Each of them had one whack of the ball from 100 yards to get it on the green and the closest ball to the flag won. Guess who was the champion while shooting from the Paramobile? Anthony! He swings with his arms to drive because he cannot turn his torso or transfer his weight. He has sent the ball over 303 yards before in one drive, almost as well as some of the best in the sport. He does not play in PGA tournaments.

Anthony now lives some in San Diego, where golf is great to play year-round, some in Florida, and he travels. He spends his time teaching about his Paramobile, which he loves. He particularly likes working with veterans and kids. He knows that to get better, 12-year-old kids with disabilities will keep up with their physical therapy, but realizes teenagers just want to hang out with friends and play video games. Unfortunately, this means the young person's health does not fare as well. A person with disabilities needs his physical therapy to keep himself in shape; so that his muscles and ligaments do not atrophy (waste away), possibly resulting in further operations. Anthony thought that if he could get teenagers interested in using his Paramobile through sports, he might be able to help them avoid these operations and continue the healthy growth of their bodies. They, in turn, would hopefully learn to love their sport and return to physical therapy. It has been medically proven that the Paramobile helps nerves regenerate. Even if someone does not want to play golf, the Paramobile can be used for modified tennis, baseball, table tennis, archery, and basketball, among other sports. So Anthony travels around teaching kids how to use it. It is one of his favorite pastimes.

Section I   The Athletes

Here are two stories Anthony loves to tell about some of his experiences. Anthony may be serious about his Paramobile, but he can be a jokester when it comes to his lessons. He told one boy who had disabilities that if the boy took a shot and then attempted to scoot away in the cart, leaving Anthony in the boy's baby wheelchair with his leg braces, Anthony could push a button and blow up the Paramobile. The boy took the shot; zoomed 500 yards away, and then suddenly stopped, turned his head and with an expression of disbelief on his face said, "Really?" Anthony and his parents laughed.

Another time, in Germany, Anthony's heart just melted when working with a child. Kids from a local Montessori school had all come out for a Par 3 tournament, which is basically a small tournament where the children try to get the ball into each hole in three shots. The children learned to use the Paramobile, and the next day their family and friends were invited out to the course. One 14-year-old boy, who also had a slight learning disability, came over to Anthony and thanked him for the experience. He said that it was the first time his daddy had ever done anything with him. His father was an avid golfer and had come out to the course because he was inquisitive about how his son could now golf. Finally, an activity they could do together. Anthony was touched.

Anthony's dream is for every public golf course in America to have one or two Paramobiles since individuals who are paralyzed do better in golf and have better health when they stand up. There are millions of people who have disabilities that would benefit. Corporate companies can even place their own logos on them when they fund one to thank a local hero. There is no capability right now to mass-produce them, and Anthony has no intention of having them manufactured in China. Between 5 and 10 are made at one time.

Anthony never thought he would golf again when he was injured in war and then hit by a drunken driver. He will keep knocking down barriers that face those with disabilities. Will you join him? You, too, can find a window to climb through and help those with disabilities live again to their utmost.

Section I The Athletes

Anthony Netto's Story

What do you think?

1. If you were paralyzed, would you want to use a Paramobile? Why? Or why not?

2. Now that you know about the Paramobile and understand how it helps those who are paralyzed, would you be interested in having a fundraiser to buy one for your local golf club and have Anthony Netto come and do a demonstration? You can contact him through the www.Standupandplay.org foundation.

3. Do you think Anthony Netto had a lot of courage accepting his disability and looking for a way to make his life better?

4. Can you think of a barrier that athletes with disabilities still need to cross?

5. Can you think of a way to help them cross it?

6. What type of invention would you like to create to help athletes with disabilities?

7. Do you think the Paramobile can help those who are paralyzed improve their health as Anthony Netto suggests it can?

8. If you were paralyzed at age 14 or 15, would you use a Paramobile, or still hang out with friends and play video games, even if it meant you might have to have an operation to get better?

Anthony Netto's Story

Did you know?

- Anthony Netto was born in 1963 in Cape Town, South Africa.
- He started playing golf at age 5, and during the 1980s became a golf pro in between his other work. As a golf pro in South Africa, his best score was 66. His average distance was around 300 yards.
- In the early 1990s, Anthony was injured in war and was hit by a drunken driver, leaving him incompletely paralyzed below the waist and with hand problems.
- Anthony, Christian Nachtwey, and a group of engineers took 12 years to design the first Paramobile, which was completed in 2001.
- There are now over 500 Paramobiles in the world, 170 of which are in America. Veterans used 85 percent of the Paramobiles in 2015. The cost of the vehicle is subsidized by the www.Standupandplay.org foundation.
- His goal is to have one or two Paramobiles available at every public golf course and to let people know the problems of individuals who are paralyzed in not standing during sports. His aim is to teach others the benefits that standing can provide in health for those individuals.
- A golfer does not need to use any special golf clubs when using the Paramobile.
- Anthony, while using the Paramobile, has had his club head speed recorded at 221 mph, and he has hit balls over 303 yards. In 2013, his personal best round was a 2-under par 70 and even par in a fundraising tournament.
- He lives and works some in San Diego, and some in Florida, to support the work of his foundation and to take advantage of the both places' year round golfing weather as well as work with the San Diego rehabilitation program. The rest of the time he travels.
- Anthony was diagnosed with multiple sclerosis in 2001.

Section I The Athletes

Super Athlete
A Cartoon

Opening the Gate

by Rebekka Hearl

Section I The Athletes

Opening the Gate

Section II

The Activities

Section II The Activities

Hold a Carnival
Support our Athletes with Disabilities

Athletes who have disabilities work hard to do well in their sport. Their recreation centers, organizations, and events need your help to keep them functioning. You can do this by hosting a carnival at your school, church, recreation center, or in your backyard. Have a theme, such as what it is like to have disabilities and participate in sports. Then donate the money to one of these organizations or centers. You can find many of these on the web.

To put on a carnival with a group you belong to, such as a scout troop, or your friends, takes considerable planning but will be fun. Included below are some ideas on how to organize and plan the carnival, as well as what to do on the day before and after the event. There are also suggested activities, but try to come up with your own ideas. Remember, you may only be able to do a small carnival and have a few stations, unless you have a larger group, in which case you can put on a large carnival with many stations. Put on a carnival of the size that you and your group can handle and get adults to supervise on the day of the carnival, so that nobody gets hurt!

Section II   The Activities

The Carnival - Possible Activities

Wheelchair Basketball

You will need a wheelchair, a portable basketball hoop, or a stationary one at a school or driveway, a basketball, and masking tape. Put the masking tape on the concrete at three different distances from the basket. Have the carnival attendees pay to take turns trying to shoot a basket while sitting in a locked wheelchair or an ordinary chair from the taped spots. If they make one basket out of three, they receive a prize.

Bowling for Those Who are Blind

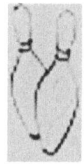 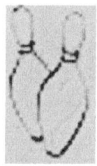

You will need some duckpins, a soccer ball, two chairs, a blindfold, and a strip of smooth plywood, or a strip of plywood with two medium sheets of thick wood.

First, you need to see if the local bowling alley is willing to donate some old duckpins. Lay a sheet of smooth plywood on the ground. Put the pins at the end of it. At the other end on either side, put the back of the chairs. You can also use sheets of thick wood that you hammer to the side of the plywood at the bottom. The tops of the sheets of wood as well as the tops of the chairs need to come to the hips of the average attendee.

To play the game, a person puts on the blindfold. With the help of the back of the chairs or sheets of wood that are used for guard rails, the player guides themselves to throw the soccer ball down the center of the lane (the plywood) and tries to knock over the pins. They get three turns to make a strike. If the player makes a strike, they receive a prize.

Floor Volleyball or Badminton

Have people sign up ahead of time for a sit-down volleyball game or a badminton tournament. If you are playing badminton, you will need a net, two or four badminton rackets, and a birdie. If you instead want the game to be volleyball, then you will need a volleyball net and volleyball. Make a chart to write down the names of the individuals as they advance to the quarterfinals, semifinals, and finals. Give prizes, such as trophies, to the victors. Look up the basic rules of volleyball and badminton and simplify them for the tournament, so it is clear how you will determine the winners.

Wiffle Ball for Those Who Are Blind

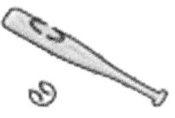
You will need a plastic bat, a wiffle ball, a blindfold, and a piece of chalk. Draw a circle on the ground with the chalk for the batter. Have the batter put on the blindfold and step into the circle. Give him the bat. Tell the pitcher to move a little ways out in the field from the batter and toss the ball directly to the player, telling the batter the whole time where and when to swing. The player who can hit the wiffle ball 5 out of 15 times wins a prize.

Modified Golf

You will need an indoor golf mat game with a club and a golf ball, or two yards of green felt, a small can, masking tape, a golf ball, and a golf club. Set up the golf mat game or your own mat game. To set up your own mat game, lay the cloth down on the ground. Tape the can at the end of the material. Mark an "X" with masking tape at the other end of the material. Tie the player's dominant arm behind his back. Give him the golf club and golf ball. He has to place the ball on the "X" and shoot the ball in the cup in five tries to receive a prize.

Section II   The Activities

Modified Football

You will need a football and two pieces of rope. Tie the non-dominant arm of each of the two participants behind his/her back. Determine how far you want them to stand apart. Give them a football, and tell them they will be working as a team. They have to pass the football 10 times. If between the two of them, they can catch it five times; they both win a prize.

Shot Puts or Javelin Throw

You will need a bar stool with a back, masking tape, a tape measure, and a softball, or a turbo javelin for this shot put or javelin throwing event. Tape the measuring tape to the ground with the masking tape. Place the bar stool at the beginning of the measuring tape. Sign people up ahead of time for this contest. The person sitting on the bar stool who throws the shot put (softball) or the javelin (turbo javelin) the farthest, wins the prize.

Learning Sign Language for Sports

Provide six chairs for this activity. You also will need two volunteers who are skilled in sign language. The volunteers will teach two people at a time how to sign five sport sentences, such as the following:

1. I like sports
2. I know how to swim
3. I am an athlete
4. I own a basketball
5. I support the (such and such organization

Afterward, the volunteers will choose three of the sentences and sign them back to one attendee at a time. If the attendee correctly understands the signing, they may have a prize.

Proper Manners Dartboard

You will need a chair, a magnetic dartboard, magnets, magnetic darts, paper, and a sharpie felt pen. Make a dartboard with one circle in the middle and five around it. The middle circle will say, "Treat with Respect, 15 points." The other circles will have the following statements: "Don't Stare," Don't Whisper About Them," "Open Doors For Them," "Help When Needed," and "Give up Your Seat." All of these will have next to them, 10 points.

Place the middle circle with a magnet in the middle of the dartboard. Put the other circles around it, a little distance away from it, and attach them with a magnet to the dartboard. Make a sign that says, "Manners to use with those who have disabilities and senior citizens." Hang the dartboard on a wall. Place the chair several yards away from it. Let the participant have five tries to make 30 points. If player does, give them a prize.

Section II   The Activities

The Carnival - Other Ideas for the Event

A Raffle

Have a raffle with the tickets costing a dollar a piece. Make sure the tickets have the phone numbers and names of the individuals.

Athletes with Disabilities Invitation

Research your area to see if any local athletes who have disabilities can come to the carnival and talk to the carnival attendees about what it is like to train, compete, etc. as an athlete with disabilities in sports.

Bake Sale

If you have a large carnival, perhaps sponsored by a larger group, like the scouts, ask an organization which works with individuals with special needs in your community if they are willing to provide an adult on their staff and two athletes with special needs who will sponsor a bake sale and drink stand. The proceeds can go towards their organization. Ask your friends to bake for it. Call some grocery stores to ask them if they will donate some drinks. Be prepared to write some nice letters to thank them afterwards.

Prostheses

Invite an athlete who has had a limb amputated to come and show your carnival participants the different prostheses he owns in order to compete in different types of sports.

Planning the Carnival

1. **Who?** - Decide whether you will put on the carnival with friends, supervised by some adults, or you will work with a group, such as the scouts or a church.

2. **Contacted Organizations that Work with Those Who Have Disabilities?** - Tell the organization that you are having a carnival to fundraise for them to help the athletes. Make sure they want you to do it for them.

3. **How big?** - Determine the size of the carnival. Remember if you are doing it in your backyard, you may only be able to have five activities at the most, whereas a scout troop with lots of volunteers can handle much more.

4. **Where?** - Decide where you are going to have the event, what day, time, and activities you will have. Make a chart with the layout of the activities and another chart for the supplies and materials you will need for each activity at the carnival.

5. **Work area?** - Designate where you will make signs, etc. for the event, and also where you will store the equipment and materials as you obtain them.

6. **Who plans?** - Decide who will be in charge of planning each part of the event.

7. **Have materials?** - Start obtaining the equipment and materials for the carnival.

Section II   The Activities

8. **The Athletes** - Contact some who have disabilities and find out if they are willing to come to the event to talk to the carnival attendees about sports and disabilities. Ask if they could tell some stories about their lives, about dealing with training issues, and competing. See if other individuals with disabilities will help out with the carnival, perhaps taking tickets at the events and answering questions about their conditions.

9. **Prizes** - Decide what prizes you will want and what you shall raffle.

10. **Tickets** - Buy or make tickets and determine how much they will cost. Obtain a moneybox for tickets and money.

11. **Money** - Decide who will be in charge of taking money for the tickets and raffle.

12. **Supervision** - Periodically check that all are doing what they need to do with his/her responsibility with the carnival.

13. **Signs & Decorations** - Decide how you are going to decorate the yard and make signs for it. For each station, you will need to make a sign with the name of the activity.

14. **Invitations and Flyers** - Decide which classmates and friends you are going to invite to the event and make flyers to give to them. If it is at your house, invite only people who you know, not strangers.

15. **Consult Adults** - Speak regularly to the adults who are supervising you. Make sure you are on track for the event. Ask them for advice on how to handle various situations.

16. **Media** - Contact the local newspaper or TV station to see if they are willing to cover the carnival the day of the event.

17. **Tables and Chairs** - Make sure you have enough for the event.

18. **Name Tags** – Print on them names of those helping with event.

19. **Notify neighbors** - Tell them that you will be holding the event. Make sure they know the date and time.

20. **First aid kit** - Acquire one, and make sure an adult who knows how to use it, is responsible for it.

Section II   The Activities

Carnival - Before the Event

1. **Bank** - Have an adult go to the bank and get the needed money and organize it in a moneybox. Make sure that during the event an adult handles the box at all times.

2. **Athletes with Disabilities** - Confirm they are coming to the event. Know at which activity they will be stationed. Suggest they either talk to the attendees, or take the tickets, or do the bake sale.

3. **Equipment and Materials** - Make sure you have all the prizes you need as well as the equipment, signs, chairs, and tables for the events.

4. **Bake** - Cook some baked goods for the bake sale and pick up drinks for the refreshment stand.

5. **Review chart** - to make sure everything is done.

6. **First Aid Kit** - Make sure you have a full kit.

7. Get a good night's sleep.

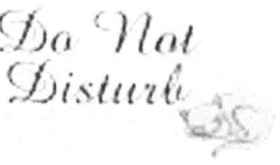
Do Not Disturb

Carnival - Day of the Event

1. **Set up** - signs, decorations, tables, chairs, games, other activities, and the raffle using your chart.

2. **Check in** - athletes, speakers, ticket takers, and helpers of the event and give each one their nametag.

3. **Check off List** - Make sure everyone is set up and has what they need. Write down anything wanted on a pad of paper.

4. **Strangers** - Keep your eyes out for anyone who does not belong and tell an adult immediately to ask the person to leave.

5. **Drinks** - Make sure everyone has water to drink, especially if it is hot.

Section II   The Activities

Carnival - After the Event

1. **Thank everyone** for attending.

2. **Clean up** - Make sure there is no trash left on the ground. Decide if you want to do the event again and then keep some of the equipment, decorations, signs, prizes, and materials for next year.

3. **Money** - Make sure you count it and immediately put it in the bank. Have an adult write a check to the organization or center for athletes with disabilities. Enclose it with a letter describing your carnival and mail the letter to the organization.

4. **Raffle** - Call the person who won the raffle and deliver the prize or ask them to pick it up.

5. **Return** - equipment, materials, tables, and chairs that you borrowed.

6. **Thank You Notes** - With your friends, write to athletes and any one who helped with the event or donated to it.

7. **Celebrate** with your friends that you did something nice for athletes with disabilities. Why not have a pizza and watch a good video?

    Sleep Soundly!

Opening the Gate

Section II   The Activities

Opening the Gate

A Matching Card Game
Know the Disabilities

In order to learn more about disabilities, it is important to know some of the terms for the athletes' medical conditions. You can then say, "Ah ha – I heard about this disability before." This matching card game can help you learn some of these terms, and it can also help you further understand how the athlete might perform in his/her sport.

What You Need:

- 20 blank 3 by 5 inch index cards
- One die
- Computer
- Sharpie felt pen

Preparations:

1. First, you will need to make two sets of cards. Write the following words on your 3 by 5 blank cards.

   a. Monochromacy
   b. Little Person
   c. Paralysis
   d. Paraplegia
   e. Cerebral Palsy
   f. Muscular Dystrophy
   g. Amputated
   h. Presbyopia
   i. Stuttering
   j. Club foot

2. Then, on the remaining 3 x 5 cards, write the definitions on the next page.

Section II   The Activities

Definitions to Write on the 3 by 5 Cards:

a. When a person can see only shades of gray instead of colors.

b. A person with stunted growth.

c. When a person cannot move a body part because of injury or disease to their nerves, or spinal cord.

d. When a person has paralysis in the lower part of the body, including the legs.

e. When a baby's brain is harmed during or a little after their birth, resulting in them having speech problems and a lack of coordination.

f. A person inherits a condition that produces muscle weakness. They cannot move well, gradually getting worse over time.

g. When at least one major joint in a limb, like a wrist, ankle, elbow, or knee has been surgically removed.

h. A medical condition where a person finds it difficult to focus on near objects.

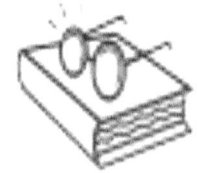

i. To speak with an involuntary disruption.

j. When a baby is born with one or two feet rotating inward at the ankle.

Opening the Gate

Instructions:

1. Now mix up all the cards and lay them upside down and spread out on the table.

2. Each player then rolls the die. The person who rolls a number closest to "6" goes first, then "5" goes second, etc. If there is a tie, the two roll again.

3. The first player then takes their turn and picks up two cards. If they pick up a word and a matching definition and recognize that the two match, they keep the set and have another turn. If not, it is the next person's turn.

4. If you need to use it - an answer sheet is included on the next page.

5. The game is over when all the sets are gone. The person winning the most sets of cards wins the game.

Once the players know all the matches, you can research new names of disabilities and their definitions. Create new cards for another game.

Have Fun!

Section II   The Activities

The Answer Sheet – Know the Disabilities

a. **Monochromacy:** When a person can see only shades of gray instead of colors.

b. **Little Person:** A person with stunted growth.

c. **Paralysis:** When a person cannot move a body part because of injury or disease to his/her nerves, or spinal cord.

d. **Paraplegia:** When a person has paralysis in the lower part of the body, including the legs.

e. **Cerebral Palsy:** When a baby's brain is harmed during or a little after his/her birth, resulting in them having speech problems and a lack of coordination.

f. **Muscular Dystrophy:** A person inherits a condition that produces muscle weakness. They cannot move well, gradually getting worse over time.

g. **Amputated:** The loss of at least one major joint in a limb from surgically cutting it off. For example: a wrist, ankle, or knee.

h. **Presbyopia:** A medical condition where a person finds it difficult to focus on objects close to them.

i. **Stuttering:** To speak with an involuntary disruption.

j. **Club Foot:** When a baby is born with one or two feet rotating inward at the ankle.

Opening the Gate

Section II   The Activities

What is it Like to Have a Disability in Sports?

To truly understand how those with disabilities perform in sports, you must try to experience their difficulties. Tie your arm behind your back. Use hand signals. Put on a blindfold while playing ball. All of these steps will help you to feel a little like these athletes. Below is a list of activities. Go out, try them with a friend and have fun while you are learning. You may discover what so many athletes with disabilities say in this book, "We can do sports well. We just do them differently."

Modified Basketball – Playing like Kevin Laue

Gather a group of friends together to play a game of modified basketball. Each of you ties your non-dominant arm behind your back. How does it feel to shoot the ball into the basket, pass, or catch the ball? Do you find yourself developing skills and techniques with only one arm? Does it get easier with time?

Mermaid in the Water – Swimming with Paralyzed Legs

What if you were in the water and had paralyzed legs, how would you tread water? Try it using only your arms. See how long you can do it. How would you get into the water? Ask your pool for permission to try to act like someone who is paralyzed getting into the pool. Most pools have a wheelchair and a mat for those with disabilities. Ask the manager if you can borrow it. First, tell him what you are doing. Pull the wheelchair up to the pool and mat. Try to get out of a locked wheelchair, like you might if your legs were paralyzed. Go down to the mat and roll yourself into shallow water, but deep enough that you do not hit the bottom, and then swim using only your arms.

Section II   The Activities

A Different Experience – Watching a Game without Sight or Hearing

Take a notebook and pencil to a game you do not know at a place, such as a school or a park. Put earplugs in your ears. Try to figure out the game by only observing it. Write down its rules. Then go to a different type of game and wear a blindfold and do the same thing except bring a tape recorder this time to record what you believe is how the game is played.

Gymnastics – with a Disability Twist

Try some gymnastic tumbling moves with adult supervision by replicating various disabilities. For instance, perform a handstand with one knee down to have the feeling a little of someone with only one leg. Do a somersault with one arm behind your back. Then perform a cartwheel or roll wearing a blindfold. Be careful - perform the stunt only if you know how. You do not want to harm yourself.

An Ice Skating Challenge – Blindfolded

If you do this activity at a skating rink, make sure you already know how to skate and that you have permission from the owner or manager. Explain that you are trying to better understand disabilities - in these cases, a skater who is visually impaired and a skater who only walks on his/her toes and not flat-footed. You must have a partner for these two activities - use a blindfold for the first one. One of you wears the blindfold while the other person holds onto you. Skate around the rink blindfolded. How different is it to skate when you are not able to see? Let your partner have a turn.

Opening the Gate

Another Ice Skating Challenge - on Your Toes

The second activity is to understand a skater who walks on his/her toes instead of flat-footed. Hold onto your partner for this activity. Go around the rink on the tip picks of your skates, which is the silver toe part of the skate. Is it hard to do? How soon do you become tired?

Wrestling Blindfold – with Style

Try wrestling blindfolded. Move all the furniture around you. You do not want to hurt yourself. Some wrestlers have legs that are paralyzed, or they only have one leg. Have someone tie your legs together while you are on the ground and then try to wrestle each other. Start on your knees. Then have someone tie one of your arms behind your back and try to wrestle.

"I'm Going to Beat You" – Speedo Wheelchairs

Obtain two wheelchairs for a race at the track against your friend. Understand the wheelchairs are different than ones which racers with disabilities use. Have an adult supervise you. How well did you do? How much arm strength did you need to perform the task?

Badminton for Hearing Impaired – Using Hand Communication

Ask your friends over for a game of badminton. Tell them that they can only talk using their hands. If they speak, they must sit out for five minutes to penalize their side.

Section II   The Activities

An Eventful Visit – Observing Athletes with Disabilities in Action

Find a local sports club or organization for those with disabilities. Call the director to ask him/her if you can visit with an adult and observe the athletes performing sports. Some of the teams with athletes who have disabilities, such as some wheelchair basketball teams, may be willing to visit your school and perform a demonstration for you. It is possible they may play against your school basketball team.

"Shh, Quiet! – I'm Watching Beep Baseball"

Search online for the national beep baseball association (nbba.org) for those who are visually impaired and try to find out if there is a team playing locally. Call the secretary of the NBBA, or the captain of the local team, and ask if you can observe a game with an adult. If they say "yes," make sure you are quiet at the game. Those who are visually impaired can become distracted with noises and may not be able to hear the ball. Because they cannot see, they are hearing sensitive.

Signing Your Way to a Touchdown – with Hand Signals

William "Dummy" Hoy was the first player who was hearing impaired in Major League Baseball. He could not understand the umpire when he called balls and strikes. He invented hand signals still used today, so the umpires could sign instead. Play a game of football with your friends wearing earplugs and use only hand signals for "unsportsmanlike conduct," "play on" and "first down." Use a drum for hut 1, hut 2, because those who are hearing impaired can hear vibrations but not words. No one is allowed to speak.

Opening the Gate

Cool Sports Equipment – for Those Who Have Disabilities

Many local Park and Recreation departments have programs for those who have disabilities, as well as equipment that are used by them in sports, such as hand cycles. With an adult, you may be able to call one of the program directors and get permission to observe how some of the equipment is used and even try it.

Flying High – Modified Frisbee

Play Frisbee with a friend with your dominant hand tied behind your back.

Youtube – Riveted by the Athlete Who Has Disabilities

Watch videos on Youtube.com on various sports performed by athletes who have disabilities, such as wheelchair tennis, wheelchair table tennis, all sorts of track and field, etc. Search online for athletes who have disabilities, or look up the sport in which an athlete with disabilities is potentially participating.

Volunteer – Cheering on Those with Special Needs

When you are 14 years old, you can volunteer to work with athletes who have special needs at the Special Olympics.

What did you learn from doing these activities that helped you understand the athlete with disabilities better?

Section II   The Activities

Section III

Further Information

Section III Further Information

Ways to Adapt Sports for Athletes with Disabilities

People with disabilities can perform most sports along with athletes who have no physical disabilities if modifications are made to the equipment, the environment, the rules, or the training of the athlete with disabilities. Below are some examples of how sports can be adapted to allow those who have disabilities to participate; however, there are dozens more. After reading the list, can you think of some modifications you can make to other sports to enable those with disabilities to compete in them, too?

Alpine Skiing
1. Provide a guide without disabilities to assist the skier who is visually impaired.
2. Allow an athlete who has disabilities to use a sit-ski or a mono-ski.

Archery
1. Provide a stool to sit on for the athlete.
2. Give a mechanical release to an archer with one arm.

Bowling
1. Allow the athlete with disabilities to use two hands for the ball.
2. Provide guardrails or special bumpers for the athlete who is visually impaired.

Golf
1. Allow the use of a club with a larger head and colored balls.
2. Let the athlete use a tee for all hits.

Indoor Soccer
1. Play with two teams of power wheelchairs on a regular basketball court with a 13-inch soccer ball.
2. Change the number of people playing on each side.

Section III   Further Information

Outdoor Soccer
1. Provide crutches for athletes who are disabled that need them.
2. Equip the ball with a noise-making device for athletes who have visual impairments.

Running
1. Allow an individual who has had a limb amputated to use a bladed prosthesis. These have been ruled legal for the athlete who is disabled as it does not provide an "extra spring" in his/her step.
2. Allow an athlete with visual impairments to be guided by a runner having no disabilities with ropes held loosely between the second and third fingers.

Softball
1. Provide Velcro balls and mitts.
2. Allow the athlete to use a batting tee to hit the ball.

Surfing
1. Equip the individual with a limb amputated with a special waterproof prosthesis.
2. Allow those with disabilities to use special boards ranging from a lay-down paddleboard to the wave-ski, which is a surfboard with a seat.

Swimming
1. Equip pools with chair lifts and built-in ramps to help athletes with disabilities enter and exit water.
2. Allow athletes with disabilities to enter the pool in their own way, instead of diving during practice and competitions.

Tennis
1. Allow a two-bounce rule for the ball for the athlete with disabilities while the other tennis players are only permitted one bounce in returning the ball.
2. Provide a larger head racket and a brightly colored ball.

Volleyball

1. Allow lowering of the nets and the use of a larger ball.
2. Provide those who are hearing impaired with interpreters to play the game.

Working out at gyms

1. Add back supports to weight lifting equipment.
2. Add toe straps to cardio equipment.

Section III   Further Information

Quotes about Disabilities
From Athletes & Others

"Find a coach who believes in you. Don't find one who is negative."

"If you try one way, and it doesn't work; try another way."

"I would fall a lot during walking and training and just go on and pretend like nothing happened."

Hannah McFadden
(Paralympic wheelchair track racer)

"When someone writes 'disability,' they should cross out the 'dis' and keep the 'ability' because I think that everyone is able to do something."

"Sports are my passion. Paving access to others is my purpose."

Tatyana McFadden
(Paralympic wheelchair track racer)

"Every parent should say to a child, 'How can I help you to be the best you can be."

"When you are comfortable with your disability, others are too."

"It may be hard to see a child struggle, but it will help her do something else."

Deborah McFadden
(Hannah and Tatyana's mother)

"It is natural with kids to be more curious. They don't understand my problem. Adults should have more respect."

"I want anyone with a disability to be able to say, 'If she can do that, I can do something else.'"

Jessica Long
(Paralympic swimmer with lower limbs amputated)

Section III   Further Information

"You have to be willing to fail, but not willing to accept failure."

Nick Taylor
(Paralympic wheelchair tennis player)

"It's the ability, not the disability, which makes a good golfer."

"Everyone has a disability in golf, even if not physical."

"Learning to hit the ball far or into the hole…that's what it is about and not learning about your missing arm, or leg, or aches, or pains."

"Some people are scared about disabilities because they are afraid it might happen to them."

Anthony Netto
(Golf player who is paralyzed)

"Promise me you'll always remember: you're braver than you believe, and stronger than you seem, and smarter than you think."

    A.A. Milne in Winnie-the-Pooh as said by Christopher Robin

"When God closes a door, he opens a window."

"There will come a time when you will want to quit; the question is, will you?"

Anonymous Sources

"The blind do not need pampering."

Stephen Guerra
(Secretary of the National Beep Baseball Association)

Websites & Organisations

Here you can find further information about the athletes, the organizations in this book, how to donate and what else you can do to help their cause.

The Athletes:

Greg Gontaryk
If you would like to donate to the National Beep Baseball Association, which is one of his causes, you will find the website info on the next page.

Kevin Laue
Learn about the 2013 Oscar-qualifying documentary about Kevin's teen years as a basketball player as well as his story of playing with one arm through the web site www.thekevinlauestory.com. You can now book Kevin for youth, corporate, and spiritual speaking engagements through www.kevinlaue.net.

Jessica Long
You can find information and news about Jessica on her facebook page at www.facebook.com/pages/Jessica-Long17959176479 or twitter.com/jessicalong.

Anthony Netto
If you would like to donate to The Stand Up And Play Foundation, which is one of his causes, you will find the website info on the next page.

Hannah McFadden
You can find information and photos on Hannah at this site,
www.hannahmcfadden.com

Nick Taylor
You can see Nick play on YouTube. If you would like to donate to Wheelchair Sports, which is one of his causes, you will find the website info on the next page.

Section III   Further Information

Some Organizations:

Adaptive Sports Association in Durango, Colorado

This organization provided the cover photo of the book. It offers year-round sports and recreational opportunities to people with physical and cognitive disabilities.

www.asadurango.org

National Beep Baseball Association

This is the organization that Greg Gontaryk supports. The website has tons of information about the game of beep baseball: from its history to its rules, as well as photos of the World Series and the teams that participated.

www.nbba.org

The Paralympic Movement

This is the official website of the Paralympic movement. Here you can find all sorts of information about its games, athletes involved, results, and rankings, among other tidbits. Many of the athletes written about in this book have participated in the Paralympics.

www.paralympic.org

The Stand Up And Play Foundation

Anthony Netto helped formed this organization for individuals with impaired mobility stand up and participate in sporting, artistic, and other daily events. Its goal is to have Paramobiles and other mobility devices available to organizations, golf clubs, and individuals everywhere. It is 100 percent run by volunteers, and 100 percent of its donations go for its endeavor.

www.stand-up-and-play.org

Wheelchair Sports, Inc.

This is a nonprofit corporation located in Wichita, Kansas, dedicated to the promotion of adaptive sports and recreation in South Central Kansas. Nick Taylor is the vice president of the corporation. The organization is a chapter of Disabled Sports, USA. You can donate to one of Nick Taylor's causes on the web site, http://www.wcsports.org.

Section III   Further Information

Acknowledgments

We would like to thank the following for their contributions to this book and those that encouraged us in our writing endeavors.

For help with the conception of the book: Ryan Swailes, Julie Barefoot and Tom Barefoot. For allowing us to write their stories: Hannah McFadden, Nick Taylor, Kevin Laue, Jessica Long, Greg Gontaryk, Anthony Netto, Tatyana McFadden and Cole Perez. For help with the publishing process and wonderful ideas: Kristin Gillern, Tom Gillern and Kari Di Luzio. For editing: Colonel William E. Rawlinson, Jr., Mary Anne Rawlinson, Dr. Winsome Leslie, Betty Jean Allison and Nicola Di Luzio. For help with obtaining athletes, other professionals and photographs for the book and giving information about the athletes: Steve Dombrosky, Amanda Korba, Andrew Barranco, Deborah McFadden, John Lykowski Jr., Joseph Clifford, Stephen Guerra, Steve Long, Melody Rafiei, Lee Hagar, Scott Perez, Patricia Sanders-Perez, Elizabeth Blair Ruder and Bob Memory. For their ideas and feedback about the whole project: Eric Halfpap and Robert McFall. For his ideas for a cartoon: Jason Barefoot. For their knowledge about medical conditions and sports psychology: Dr. Basil Morgan, Dr. James McGee and Dr. Harold Steinitz. For the many children and adults who read the stories and gave us their feedback: Robert Di Luzio, Marc Di Luzio, Shane Gillern, Nora Gillern, Holly Mihok, Olivia Mihok, Jennifer King, Asia Byrd, Akihbah Byrd, Alijujuan Byrd, Charlie Halfpap, Aidan Halfpap, Elizabeth Grefe, Nicholas Grefe, Sarah Grefe, Noelle Leslie, Kevin Treakle, Paul Conrad, Pam Howard and Betsy. For those who have encouraged me on this project and my writing throughout many years: Richard Martin, Lynn Perrott, Dr. Beatrice Taylor, Jeff Zemenick, Sharon Bartsch, Erik Floyd, Paul Floyd, Dr. Suzanne Griffin and Sr. Marie Charles,

And thanks to the many organizations that gave us ideas for activities so that children with no physical disabilities could better understand how those with disabilities participate in sports.

Section III   Further Information

About Us

Ingrid Floyd, the author, is from Arlington, Virginia, and now lives in Towson, Maryland. She has worked with children of all ages for over 35 years and loves her work. She has a degree in Elementary Education from Towson University and also attended University of Virginia for her undergraduate courses. She is a journalist and has had over 50 articles published. In her twenties, she taught gymnastics at Midatlantic Gymnastics Center in Baltimore, Maryland. She has taken classes at Towson University in physical education, and in high school for three years, she worked with those that had special needs at a summer camp. You can contact Ingrid Floyd at her Facebook address, https://www.facebook.com/ingrid.floyd.92.

Tom Bartsch was instrumental in the conception and follow-through of this project with ideas and editorial support. He is from Waupaca, Wisconsin. A Journalism major from the University of Wisconsin-Oshkosh, he has worked at F+W Media for 15 years encompassing a variety of editorial roles. He currently serves as the editor of *Sports Collectors Digest* magazine and editorial director of the Antiques & Collectibles community at F+W Media. A life-long sports fan, you can bet he is always cheering on his beloved Milwaukee Brewers. Contact him at tommybartsch@yahoo.com.

Rebekka Hearl has designed the cartoon. She has a BA (Hons) in Computer Visualization and Animation from Bournemouth University in Dorset, England. She is skilled at working in both traditional and digital media in both art and illustration, as a story and comic artist, and a 2D and 3D animator. Her beloved Monster Boy, a free-to-read web comic is on her website, http://rebekkahearl.carbonmade.com

Made in the USA
Middletown, DE
20 October 2025